FROM THE ORGANISER

CW00520680

"Steve is the international autl
planners. His expertise and insights on brands, models, sizes and
mechanisms is unparalleled.

It has been my pleasure to collaborate with him in the last decade, be it
for designing new models, brainstorming about best practices or
organizing the first international planner convention in Europe." —
Mella Pieper, CEO of PlannerCon Europe

———

"I have been working with Steve for several years, managing social
media groups about planning and Filofax. I cannot think of anyone more
qualified to write a Filofax Guidebook." — Alan Marshall, Canada

———

What sets Steve Morton apart is not simply his encyclopaedic knowledge
of all things Filofax (and planners too), but his generosity in sharing that
knowledge in a genuine desire to help, support and develop the whole
planner community. — David Round, William Hannah Limited

———

"Steve is my go-to person when I have any planner related questions.
Not only does he know everything about this topic, but also his expertise
is as great as his enthusiasm, which makes his book a highly enjoyable
read and gives him the status of planner guru." — Petra Van der Spek,
CEO Van der Spek Leather Goods, Netherlands

ABOUT THE AUTHOR

Steve Morton was born and raised in northwest England and worked as a specialist radio engineer for 35 years before retiring in 2010. A change of job in 2005 to a security-conscious environment meant he returned to a Filofax. He has used one daily ever since. Now, he dedicates his time to writing on the Philofaxy blog and continuing with photography, radio and technology.

Steve was invited to contribute to the 2015 book *Dull Men of Great Britain* (published by Random House) as a 'Filofax Blogger'.

Since 2016 he co-hosts a podcast with Karine Tovmassian – *The Hitchhikers Guide to the Plannerverse* – devoted to making better use of planners and organisers.

He lives with his author wife Alison in their house in France, enjoying the slower pace of life.

Join him at the Philofaxy blog: https://philofaxy.blogspot.com

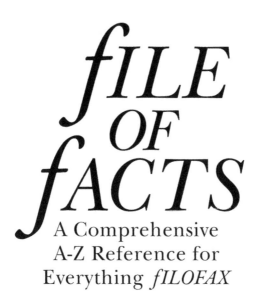

*f*ILE
OF
*f*ACTS

A Comprehensive
A-Z Reference for
Everything *f*ILOFAX

Steve Morton

PULCHERIA
PRESS

Cover design by Avalon Graphics

ISBN 9791097310332 (ebook)
ISBN 9791097310325 (paperback)

CONTENTS

INTRODUCTION

In the era of connected devices and the Internet, the reason why you choose to use a Filofax in the 21st century is very much a personal one. You will often hear people say, "Oh, I had one of those" or "I still have one of those somewhere".

However, please don't think you have to provide an excuse for using a Filofax. For most of us the decision was simple; it's an uncomplicated solution to managing daily productivity and time. You don't need a signal or power source, just a pen and your organiser with some paper inside.

For people just starting to use a Filofax or other brand of ring-bound organiser (Gillio, Van der Spek), you might be confused by some of the phrases and terminology that people use when you enter the planner community.

For a few years, I've been wanting to do an A-Z of Filofax, working through the alphabet, picking out terminology and providing helpful hints and fun facts.

I've also provided a chronology of the company and the history of ring-bound planners through the decades.

Let's get started.

IMPORTANT NOTE

Filofax is a registered trademark of FLB Group (Filofax Letts Blueline Group), and the word Filofax may only be used to describe products manufactured by Filofax.

Other trade names quoted in this book are registered by their respective owners and have no connection with Filofax.

This informal guide is written by a fan, an amateur (although knowledgeable) enthusiast who has no connection with the current owners of Filofax.

A

A4 A5 A6

These are all ISO (International Standards Organisation) paper sizes, see ISO216. Each one is in the same proportion of 1:1.4142, A4 is twice the size of A5, A5 is twice the size of A6, etc. (1.4142 is the square root of 2.) That is as deep into maths as we will be going in this book!

These three are the most common page sizes you will find for organisers. Filofax make A4 and A5 size organisers, but they never imported A4 ones to the USA. The A6 isn't sold by Filofax as it falls between Personal size and Pocket size. You will find A6 size organisers sold by Van der Spek (called Senior), Gillio, Mulberry and others.

Their pages sizes are as follows:

A4 – 297mm x 210 mm

A5 – 210mm x 148 mm

A6 – 148mm x 105 mm

Although Filofax has never made an A6 size organiser, you will often see Personal size described as A6 size. This is incorrect. If in doubt, check the page dimensions.

Address

Keeping addresses in your organiser was, and still is for some users, one of the main advantages of a ring-bound organiser over a bound planner. You can simply replace the diary section each year and only need to update the address book pages or replace them as and when there are major updates and alterations.

How many addresses you store in your organiser is, of course, up to you. You can store all of them or just the ones that you frequently need to access. Some users even have a separate index for people on their Christmas card list.

Address pages come in various formats; some just contain essential name, mailing address, phone number. But in this modern era, you might want to look for pages with additional information lines for email address, mobile number and maybe social media usernames.

Archive

You don't need to keep all your pages in your organiser all the time. This is one of the main advantages of a ring bound organiser in that you can swap pages in and out of the organiser as you need them. It's considered good practice to archive pages into a storage binder when you are not using them, or for long term storage.

B

Bags

Filofax in the past made some very high-quality bags for everyday use, including messenger bags and computer bags. Sadly, these disappeared from the product line in recent years.

For bags, you might like to look at Laurige France, which is linked from the Filofax UK site.

Business Card Holder

Business card slots are a relatively new feature on Filofax organisers. Back in the 1980s when credit cards became more prevalent, Filofax added a business card holder made of leather which slotted onto the rings of your personal organiser.

These vintage items are highly sought after as modern equivalents are made from plastic which only have a finite life in comparison to leather.

C

Card slot

A slot pocket for business or credit cards, either horizontal or vertical slots depending on the organiser model or size.

Care

Looking after your organiser is not too difficult. Check the organiser manufacturer's website for care information. Where possible, I recommend testing any care products on a part of your organiser that will not be easily seen. Alternatively, test the products on a leather sample first.

Clasp

The closure for your organiser, usually a tab fixed on one side with a popper (press-stud) on the other to secure it. Some organisers use a zip as an alternative. There are a few slimlines that do not have a clasp and some models that use an elastic as a closure.

Coin holder

A leather accessory that fits on the rings as a pocket to hold a *small* amount of change.

Concorde

If you'd been a First-Class VIP passenger on a British Airways 3½ hour flight between London and New York on board the Concorde aircraft, you'd have been presented with a Slimline Filofax specially made for the flight.

It had the outline of Concorde embossed into the cover in addition to the Filofax logo on the spine. The cover was in charcoal leather and the interior featured a burgundy satin lining.

Cotton cream

Higher quality paper in an ivory off-white colour, sold by Filofax

D

Dashboard

This tends to be the first item you see when you open your personal organiser. It can be made of card or laminated paper. Sometimes it features a favourite photograph or design. The laminated plastic versions can be used for adhering sticky notes.

Diary Dividers

Card or thicker paper used to divide your year into months; the tabs are often labelled with the months of the year.

Diary Insert

These inserts are probably the most often used set of pages on an hourly/daily basis. There are many different formats, but they are nearly all divided into the standard divisions of time.

- Daily
- Weekly
- Monthly
- Yearly

Disc-bound Notebooks/Planners

There are advantages to a disc-bound rather than ring-bound cover. You can still remove and replace pages easily but without the rings getting in the way of your hand when writing.

Duplex

Duplex organisers have two sets of rings; these are arranged parallel to each other. There are two versions – a narrow and a wide. In the narrow version, three pages are visible when open, but in the wider version, you can see all four pages. However, when either organiser is closed, the two sets of pages inevitably overlap.

E

eBay

A well-known auction website, a useful source for finding previously discontinued personal organisers that are no longer sold in the usual retail outlets. Visit with caution!

Emergency Information

The Emergency Information page is often the first page people will see when opening their organiser. It might contain name and address details of the owner as well as emergency contact information, such as doctor's name, partner's contact details, etc.

Be careful about how much information you store on this page in case you should lose your organiser, as it will let others find personal information about you.

Envelopes

Envelopes for your organiser were once real paper envelopes punched with a flap to hold them in. These days they come in a hard-wearing plastic or paper and can be used to hold photographs, storing receipts and other odd pieces of paper that you don't want to lose, or don't want to punch to fit onto the rings in the conventional way.

Everest

The 1976 British Army expedition to climb Mount Everest used the Filofax system as a data book for the climbers. Filofax publicised this in a magazine advertisement under the banner 'The British Filofax System has been everywhere' with images of Everest and the various staging camps on the mountain.

Expenses

As the name suggests, these inserts are used often by business people for recording expenses or for people in roles where they can reclaim out of pocket expenses.

F

Films

Filofax organisers have appeared as props in many films and TV shows. The list is constantly growing and too long to include in this section of the book, but see https://thisbugslife.com/2016/05/03/the-ultimate-compilation-of-films-featuring-filofaxes/

FiloWiki

Wikipedia for everything Filofax. This project, devised by Robert Mayr, has gathered together a wealth of information about Filofax models through the history of the company. Find it at: http://filowiki.robert-mayr.com

Filo-Fiction

Several books have been published with Filofax style pages for people to read.

Finance Pages

These are inserts used for keeping track of your personal finances, expenses, savings, etc.

Flatability

The ability of an organiser to lay flat when opened. Some organisers require 'training' to achieve the perfect 'flatability' score.

Flex

A range of Filofax notebook covers released in Spring 2011. They included a range of diary inserts, notebooks, and other accessories. They were made in A5, Slim and Pocket sizes. Sadly, now discontinued.

Flyleaf

Similar to a dashboard but often made of leather, it can feature additional card slots or a zipped pocket. Plain ones serve to smooth out the writing surface for the pages sitting over cards and other paperwork in the front pockets.

Franklin Covey

Franklin Covey, or Franklin Planner as it is now known, is an American planner company. They make ring bound and coil bound planners and use slightly different paper sizes to Filofax.

Franklin Covey Sizes		
Monarch	216 x 280mm (Letter size)	7 rings spaced 25/57mm
Classic	140 x 216mm (Half Letter size)	7 rings spaced 25/19mm
Compact	108 x 172mm (13mm wider than Filofax Personal size)	6 rings the same as Personal ring spacing 19/51mm
Pocket	89 x 153mm (Narrower than Filofax Personal size)	6 rings the same as A6 ring spacing 19/38mm

When it comes to the ring spacing, Compact is the only size the same as any of the Filofax sizes. Franklin Covey Pocket will fit an A6 organiser.

The following diagram shows in graphic form the differences between Filofax and Franklin Covey punched layouts.

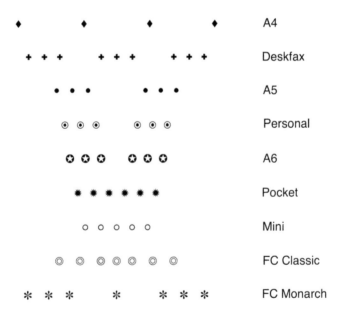

G

Getting Things Done (GTD)

A personal productivity methodology that defines how you approach your life and work, developed by David Allen and published in a book of the same name in 2001. It splits things down into five steps to help you achieve your goals. You can use a Filofax organiser for GTD.

Gillio

Gillio Firenze is a small family business that sells high-end, top quality, handmade leather goods made from the finest Italian leathers. The company started with a small stationery shop in Brussels in 1952 and they have since expanded their brand and collections significantly. Their products are sold worldwide (to almost 50 countries) online from their website.

Website: www.gillio.be

Grace Scurr (1894 – 1987)

In 1921, Grace went to work for Norman & Hill, a firm of printers and stationers in London. They imported personal filing systems from Letts of Philadelphia, United States. She suggested the name Filofax in 1925 and persuaded the firm to make the files themselves. The Filofax brand was registered as a trademark in 1930.

During the Second World War, the offices of Norman & Hill in Aldersgate Street were bombed and all records were lost with everything being destroyed. Fortunately, Grace Scurr kept a record of all their customers and suppliers in her own duplex Filofax that she took home each night, and this enabled the company to get back up and running from new offices in Watford very quickly.

Grace rose to become chairman of Filofax and had a 15% shareholding in the company. She retired in 1955 but continued as chairman for several more years. She lived in the seaside town of Southend until her death in May 1987. She had sold her shares in the company in 1982.

In 1996, to commemorate her and to celebrate 75 successful years of the company, Filofax released a limited-edition duplex Filofax based on the same design used by Grace Scurr herself. In all, 1921 examples were sold worldwide reflecting the year when the company started selling organisers.

The 'Grace Scurr' limited edition was sold in a wooden box with special edition inserts contained in the velvet lining. The organiser was displayed in the open position above the inserts. A certificate showing the number of each individual organiser was affixed inside the box lid. That same number was embossed in the front inside cover of the organiser.

The gold-plated ring mechanisms are embossed with the number '75' and engraved with 1921-1996 below that.

H

Holborn

A Filofax model from 2010 available in Pocket, Slimline, Compact, Personal, Personal Zip and A5 Zip. Please note: Holborn is pronounced "Ho-bun" not "Holl-borne"

Hole Spacing

This is the spacing between the rings. It can also be called ring spacing. The dimension is the distance between the centre of the holes or the same two points on the holes.

I

Ilford

The main office and factory for Filofax was in Forest Road, Ilford in Essex for several years. There is no trace of Filofax on the exterior of the building today. The factory workforce was reduced significantly in 1993 with production being transferred overseas.

Inserts

The pages used to record your notes and information. Filofax once sold over a thousand different specialist inserts for business, the professions, military, church and other users. The book *Filofax Facts* by Ian Sinclair features most of the range of inserts that were available in the 1980s.

Inserts included:

General Leaves

• Dated Diaries

• Undated Diaries

• Address and Telephone

- Classified Addresses
- Name, Address, Telephone
- Telephone, Name, Code

- Entertaining

  - Function Planner
  - Home Entertainment
  - Restaurant

- Health and Good Looks

  - Develop Your Wardrobe
  - Discover Your Colours
  - Guide to Additives and Vitamins
  - Slimming Calorie Counter
  - Sport and Fitness in London

- Horoscopes

- Household

  - Recipe Record
  - Shopping List
  - Telephone Message

- Leisure and Hobbies

  - Bird Watcher's Checklist
  - Bridge Score Sheet
  - Cellar Notes
  - Chess Score Record
  - Wine Tasting Record

- Memorandum

  - Don't Forget

- Enquiry
- Memo
- Notepad
- Special Reminder Record

• Private Information

  - Bibliofile
  - Birthday / Anniversary Record
  - Cards and Gifts
  - Daily Intake Record
  - Hotel
  - Most Used Telephone Numbers
  - Personal Contact Record
  - Personal Services
  - Traveller's Checklist

• Sport

  - Angler's Catch List
  - Golf Record
  - Running Record
  - Skiing Record
  - Snooker Record
  - Squash Record
  - Windsurfing Record

• Study / Revision Aids

Professional and Business Leaves

• Analysis and Cash

  - Analysis in various formats
  - Bank Account
  - Petty Cash

- Art and Design

  - Isometric
  - Music Manuscript
  - Photo Exposure Record
  - Photographer's Record
  - Photo Mounts
  - Tracing Paper

- Business Records

  - Credit Card Charges
  - Employee Record
  - Enquiry
  - Meetings Record
  - Motor Running Expenses
  - Personal Expenses
  - Petty Cash
  - Production Schedule
  - Stock Record
  - Statistics Leaf
  - Telephone Message Pad
  - Travel Itinerary

- Church

  - Church Family Record

- Education

  - Class record

- Free Form Time Management

  - Keypoints Reminders
  - Communicating Effectively

- Effective Delegation
- Finding More Time
- Managing Meetings
- Managing Paperwork
- Managing Pressure
- Problem Solving
- Productive Thinking
- Thinking Ahead

- Investments

  - Investment Annual Record
  - Investment Ledger
  - Portfoliofax Starter Pack

- Medical

  - Physician's Case Record

- Military and Marine

  - Commander's Interview Record
  - Course Bids
  - Course Instructor's Record
  - Grouping / Range Card
  - Lesson Plan
  - Marine Troop Commander's Bible
  - Platoon Commander's Personal Records
  - Sub-Unit Personnel Qualifications

- Police

  - Police Personnel Record

- Property and Surveying

- Estate Agent's Record
- Surveyor's Quantity Record

- Publishing

  - Production Schedule
  - Publication Schedule
  - Rights Negotiation Record

- Sales and Marketing

  - Customer Record
  - Enquiry

The range was rationalised in the 1990s when Robin Field took over from David Collischon to lead the company.

J

Jam Packed

We often see a 'well stuffed' organiser, full to bursting with pages and various other things in the internal pockets. However, there are potential problems with using an organiser beyond its designed capacity.

The clasp and closure can fail or, in the extreme, the clasp can become detached.

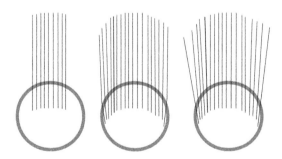

With too many pages held by the rings, the paper inside the rings can start to push the rings open. Pages can also become damaged or torn because they are not free enough to move through the rings. On small ring size organisers, the edges of the paper inside of the rings can rub up against each other and become bent over when on the opposite sides of the rings.

Rings can become distorted and pages come loose resulting in damaged or lost papers.

Jot Pad

A small note size pad punched with three holes that will fit on the rings of any Filofax organiser. Each sheet in the pad measures 85mm by 55mm. It will fit most page sizes as the three holes match the usual 19mm spacing.

Instead of a simple card backing to the pad, it has an additional flap, which can be slid into a card slot on the inside front or back cover, making the pad readily available to 'jot' something down.

K

Kensington

A Filofax model produced between 1999 and 2003 in all sizes current at the time as well as in Deskfax size. It was available in leather in six colours (black, burgundy, brown, navy, red and green) in a traditional Filofax design.

L

Lefax

Lefax was a company founded in 1910 by John Clinton Parker in Philadelphia and produced a range of personal organisers. The Lefax trademark was registered 5 October 1926. Its use in the engineering industries was so pervasive that some journals were published in Lefax format.

The name Lefax is made up from the words Leaf and Facts. Lefax at one time produced over 2500 data-sheets of single sheets printed with information for scientists, architects and engineers across the full range of industry.

In 1921, London printer and stationery marketer Norman & Hill Ltd. began importing the organisers, called Lefaxes. Several years later, they began to produce the personal files under their Filofax brand.

In the 1980s, Lefax was bought out by London Wood Partners, a British firm, and in 1992 the company was acquired by its rival, Filofax. The original intention was that Lefax would be Filofax's top of the line range, but the Lefax brand was eventually phased out.

Leather

A durable and flexible material made from the hide of animals such as cow. As a material it's been used for thousands of years to make clothing, weapons, armour, footwear, containers, furniture, bookbindings and bags of every type. Its durability is well proven and thus it has been used for personal organisers since they were first developed by Lefax in the early 1900s.

Letts

Charles Letts Group, famous for its diaries, acquired Filofax from Day Runner in 2001 for £17m. By 2003, the company was renamed Letts Filofax.

M

M2

M2 organisers have only three rings. Their page size is 103mm x 64mm in landscape format rather than portrait format which makes the page size similar to the current Filofax Mini size.

Malden

A Filofax model featuring contrast stitching and a pointed clasp that came out in 2010, initially available in only Personal and Pocket sizes. It was eventually made available in all sizes from Mini to A5. A full range of accessories was also produced in the 'Malden Style'.

Marker

A page marker can show the current day or week, so that you can quickly open your organiser at that page to make a note or add a task to your diary. Some people use more than one marker if they have a combination of Weekly/Monthly or Daily/Weekly inserts, as it helps them flip from one to the other quickly.

Meet-Up

An informal gathering of Filofax users. Steve hosted the first Philofaxy meet-up at the Tate Modern Art Gallery on 20 November 2010. There have been many others since in cities and towns around the world including those attended by Steve in UK, USA, Canada, Netherlands, Belgium, Sweden and France.

Mini

The Filofax Mini size organisers introduced in 1995, effectively replaced Filofax M2 size. The inserts are quite small, close to A7 size.

Mini inserts have 5 holes each equally spaced at 19mm apart. A Pocket page size punch can be used to punch Mini pages.

Another novel fact is that you can fit two Mini pages on to the A5 organisers rings (top three and bottom three rings) without the pages overlapping or overhanging beyond the edges of the A5

pages. You could therefore have two independent sets of inserts on view at any one time. Whilst this works in theory, I've never seen anyone use an A5 with Mini pages.

Models

For a comprehensive list of Filofax models, see List of Models and Years at the end of this book.

Moving in

The action of using an organiser for the first time. Moving your current inserts into your new organiser and putting it to use.

Mulberry

A British company established in 1971, they are mainly known for their bags, but they also make leather organisers in Pocket, A6 and A5 sizes.

Note that Mulberry A5 uses the same spacing as Filofax Personal size. Quo Vadis also uses the same spacing in their A5 organisers.

Parameter (Filofax/Mulberry)	Filofax	Mulberry
Paper size (Pocket)	120 x 81 mm	120 x 76 mm
Paper size (Personal/Agenda)	171 x 95 mm	148 x 105 mm (A6)
Paper size (A5/Planner)	210 x 148 mm	210 x 148 mm
'3 ring spacing'	19 mm	19 mm
Ring Spacing between rings 3 and 4 (Pocket)	19 mm	19 mm
Ring Spacing between rings 3 and 4 (Personal/Agenda)	51 mm	38 mm
Ring Spacing between rings 3 and 4 (A5/Planner)	70 mm	51 mm

N

Note pad

A note pad in the back of your organiser is a convenient way of writing notes without the rings of your organiser hindering your writing hand. The note can then be removed from the note pad and inserted into the appropriate section of your organiser.

You can also pass notes to colleagues easily, assuming they also use an organiser!

O

Organisers

Organisers come in a variety of sizes from Mini at one end of the scale to the A4 at the other, with several sizes in between those two extremes.

Choosing the right size of organiser to use can be a compromise and a challenge. I always recommend starting off with blank sheets of paper in the various sizes of organiser and try planning on the different size sheets for a day or two to see which size will accommodate a typical day or week for your requirements. This prevents you having either a lot of blank space (too big a page) or not enough space (too small a page).

Bear in mind how you are going to carry whichever size of organiser you will be using. Larger tends to be heavier so it's wise to check the physical size of the organiser to see if it will fit in your bag.

It's best to do some simple trials before you invest in one particular size as it will save you money in the long term. The true benefit of getting it right first time will encourage you to use your organiser to its full extent.

P

Page Lifter

A divider that helps the paper from being trapped on large rings when closing the organiser. They act to push the pages to the central arc of the rings. Typically, they have slotted holes so they also don't get trapped on the rings.

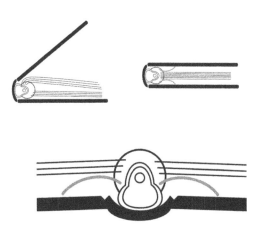

Page Sizes

These are the most popular page sizes.

Size	H x W (mm)	Rings (Number x Group)
A4	297 x 210	4
Deskfax (B5)	250 x 176	3 x 3
A5	210 x 148	3 x 2
Personal	171 x 95	3 x 2
Compact/Slimline	171 x 95	3 x 2
A6	148 x 105	3 x 2
Pocket	120 x 81	6
Mini	105 x 67	5
M2	64 x 103	3

They are all 'portrait' format except for the M2 which is 'landscape' format.

Paper

The essential ingredient in any personal organiser. The choice of paper both in quality and thickness is very wide. Finding a paper that you prefer and that works with your pen/ink combination is extremely important.

Test out samples before deciding on a particular brand or type. Take into consideration the ability of your computer printer to handle the thickness/type of paper you choose if you print your own inserts.

Paul Smith

Paul Smith is a top British fashion designer. During the 1980s he sold Filofax organisers alongside his flamboyant clothing in his London Covent Garden store. It helped the general public become aware of the Filofax brand. He subsequently produced his own brand of ring bound organisers in a variety of colourful designs.

Pens

Like paper, pens are essential; some people also use pencils. There is a vast number of different types of pens you can successfully use in any personal organiser. Use the ones that suit your purpose and pocket. Take into account the size of the pen loop on your organiser, if it has one.

Personal Size

The original size for all personal organisers, 95mm x 171mm (3.75 x 6.75 inches approx). It features six punched holes in two groups of three. The three rings are spaced at 19mm (0.75 inch) apart with 50.8 mm (2 inches) between the two groups.

Personal Wide

A new 'invented' size of paper, 121mm x 172mm (4.75 x 6.75 inches), it needs extra wide organisers to hold it.

When you look at ISO216 the International Standard for paper sizes, Personal Wide is close to B6 paper size, which is 125mm x 176mm. B6 is easier to use than Personal Wide because you can scale existing inserts in other ISO sizes to it easily. The slightly taller pages in B6 are fine in most organisers.

Filofax do not currently sell Personal Wide organisers, but they are available from other manufacturers.

Philofaxy

A well-known website dedicated to ring bound planners. the name derives from the Greek *philos* (φιλος) meaning loving or beloved. The site was started in October 2005 by a blogger in the

USA. He was later joined by Nan Barber, who by late 2006 was running the blog on her own after the original 'Philofaxer' started a family and found he had less time to devote to the blog.

Nan recruited Steve and Laurie in 2009 to help and they were joined by Anita in 2012. Between them, the team have managed to keep the blog rolling daily with posts on every possible topic you could imagine about personal organisers. There are regular posts each week that highlight posts and videos on other sites.

Philofaxy has organised several on-line events, a regular virtual meet-up on Skype most months, as well as face-to-face events in the UK and other parts of the world.

Planner Con

A bigger form of meet-up attended by hundreds of planner and organiser users. They enjoy talks and visiting trade stands, plus have the chance to meet all those other people they have only ever seen on social media.

PlannerCon USA holds events on the West coast of the USA and PlannerCon Europe has held events in Belgium.

Pocket Size

Pocket size Filofax organisers were introduced in 1989. At the time, they contained only four rings rather than the six rings we have today. Their rings had the same spacing as the four inner rings of personal size. Six-ring Pocket size organisers first appeared in 1994; these have equal 19mm ring spacing between each ring pair.

Podcast

A spoken word audio file, similar to a radio show, but one that you can download and listen to in your own time. A 'plannercast' is a podcast for the planner community.

Steve is a co-host and producer of a plannercast with Karine Tovmassian called *The Hitchhikers Guide to the Plannerverse*. Any similarity to The Hitchhiker's Guide to the Galaxy is pure coincidence!

Printer

An essential accessory together with a computer, if you want to personalise and print your own inserts rather than purchasing them pre-printed.

Punch

Paper punches come in a variety of types and sizes. Some are single page size models, others can be easily adapted to suit different Filofax ring spacings. For example, one punch can be used for Pocket, A6, Personal and A5.

A punch is an essential accessory if you are printing your own inserts.

Q

Quo Vadis

Quo Vadis is a French company better known for its bound planners and notebooks. However, they also have several organiser inserts using the 'Timer' trade name which come in A5, Personal and Pocket size.

Note that the A5 size Timer21 inserts are punched for the Quo Vadis A5 organisers which use rings with Personal spacing. Therefore, to use these in an A5 Filofax requires the pages to be re-punched.

Quality Control Letters

You might not have noticed them, but on the inside of the clasp of your Filofax organiser you may find three letters embossed into the leather. On zip closure models, the three letters are tucked away on the inside , sometimes inside a pocket or behind a flap.

These three letters indicate the year, month and location of manufacture. The first letter is the year with A indicating 1991, the second letter is the month in that year. The third letter is the location of the factory. The first letter of Z would indicate 2016.

Don't worry if you can't find the three-letter code. You don't necessarily have a fake Filofax if there isn't a code. It's not unusual for the code to be left off and quite a few of my recent Filofax organisers haven't got a code. Pre-production samples, for instance, never seem to have the code.

R

Rings

The ring size of a Filofax organiser is measured as the internal diameter in millimetres. Although the USA site converts this into inches, it's not always done accurately.

Ring Size	Organiser Size	Capacity (sheets)
30 mm	A5, Personal Zip	330
25 mm	A5 Clasp	270
23 mm	Personal Clasp	250
19 mm	Pocket	200
15 mm	Compact	150
13 mm	Slimline, Mini	120
11 mm	Slimline, Mini	105

The ring mechanism in many organisers uses a design approximately 100 years old which has hardly changed in that time.

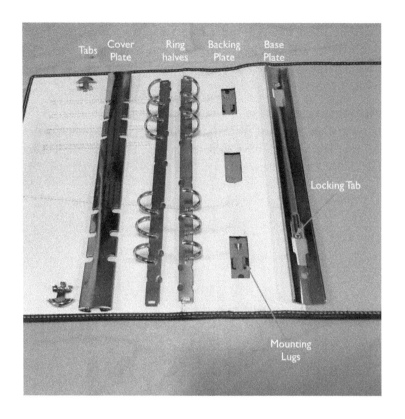

Tabs – You use these to open your rings, pressing down on both....

Cover plate – This is the part that covers up the internals of the ring mechanism and can be carefully removed without removing the ring mechanism. It clips to the base plate.

Ring Halves – When taken apart, they are in two parts but interlock when installed in the base plate. They slide in from either end of the base plate. The tabs slot into small rectangular holes at the ends.

Backing Plate – This is the metal part glued into the inside of the organiser between the outer leather and the internal leather. It's inserted before the two halves of the organiser are finally stitched together, therefore it's difficult to change this part of the mechanism. If buying replacement rings, you will normally not receive the backing plate unless you specifically ask for it.

Mounting Lugs – These are found at the top and bottom of the backing plate. The base plate slides on to these lugs. Exceptionally, A5 ring mechanisms have three mounting lugs with the locking tab on the middle one.

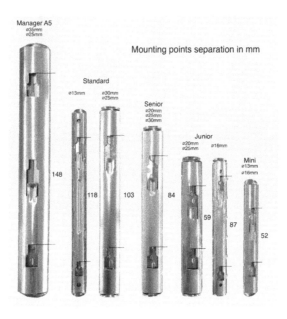

Base Plate – The ring halves are held in along with the tabs, and then the cover plate clips onto the top of the base plate.

The square cut-outs in the base plate fit on to the mounting lugs. Then you slide the base plate (and the assembled ring mechanism) onto the mounting lugs, with the narrower cut-out sliding under the mounting lugs until the locking tab clicks over the small ridge just above the lower mounting lug.

The base plate acts like a spring, keeping the ring halves together in either the open position or the closed position.

Ring mechanisms using the same method of retention in the organiser as shown in the image above are easy to change and maintain. In some instances, it's possible to change the size of the rings in the same size of organiser without changing the backplate fitted to the organiser. For example, it's possible to exchange 25mm and 30mm rings in a Personal size or 20mm and 25mm rings in an A6 organiser. The distance between the mounting lugs is the critical thing, as shown in the image on the previous page.

Older A5 ring mechanisms had two mounting lugs similar to Personal/Standard/Medium size. Modern ones have three mounting points with the locking tab in the middle cut out.

Robin Field

Filofax Chief Executive Officer from October 1990 to October 1998. During his time with the company, he pared down the range of paper inserts from 1,000 to just over 100 designs. He also cut back the product range and made other radical changes in order to reduce manufacturing costs including closing down UK production and moving it to the Far-East.

In October 1992, he oversaw the purchase of Lefax, which up until then had been considered a rival. Filofax took over the Lefax model range as well as their shops in London and Paris. Also that year, he launched the A5 Filofax and announced the nine-ring Deskfax and three-ring M2 models, although the M2 didn't appear until 2001 after he had left the company.

In June 1995, Filofax launched the Filofax Mini size of organiser and inserts.

In September 1998, the California based company Day Runner made a takeover bid for Filofax. At this point, Robin Field stood down as chairman and was succeeded by Christopher Brace.

S

Sections

Using dividers in your organiser to put your pages into different categories will help you store and retrieve information quickly.

I use the following headings for my sections:

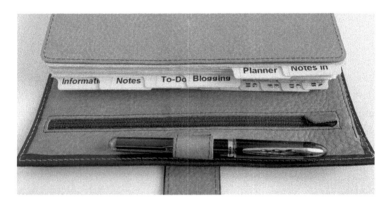

Notes In – This is a simple section with a few pages of lined paper for immediate notes to capture things on the move.

Planner – This is my Enhanced TM (time management) Week per View for all my future and daily planning requirements.

Blog Planner – I use a Month on One Page adapted to the routine schedule of the blog posts.

To-Do – These sheets are for long term goals, so I have a 'House' sheet, 'Personal' sheet, etc. On those, I list the headings and some details of things I hope to get done in the coming year.

Notes – Stuff I jot down for projects, Philofaxy posts, random websites in order to record them before I file them somewhere more appropriate.

Information – This is where I store my maps and reference information.

Address A-Z – All my contact sheets printed off from a Word document that I merge from my Apple Contacts application.

Of course, you can choose any headings you need and in any order.

Sticky Notes

Sticky notes are self-adhesive paper notes that you can remove and relocate easily on other pages. They can be useful for jotting down pieces of information quickly before putting them into the relevant page of your organiser or your diary pages for later reference.

T

Tabs

The tabs on your dividers help you find the section of your organiser you want to open. They're generally labelled with your section headings and often blank or numbered on bought dividers. You can also buy self-adhesive tabs to attach to your own dividers.

Temperley

Alice Temperley, a British fashion designer, created a range of organisers for Filofax for London Fashion Week in Spring 2012. The designs were 'different' to anything we had previously seen. According to the Filofax CEO at the time, they gained the company valuable publicity, but they weren't a wide commercial success due to the high set-up costs and the low number of actual sales at their original retail price that was considered high at the time.

Time Management (TM)

The process of organising and planning how to divide your time between specific activities. Good time management enables you to work smarter – not necessarily harder – so that you get more done in less time, even when time is tight and pressures are high. Failing to manage your time damages your effectiveness and causes stress.

Time Sheet

An insert used for recording the amount of time you spend on each job/project, generally arranged into some form of table with projects against days, sometimes hours, with a row or column for the weekly totals.

To Do Lists

A list of tasks that need to be completed, sometimes organised in the order of their priority.

Training

This is the flexing of the organiser, so it lays flat when open. To achieve this, gently bend it back beyond fully open to get the leather to 'give' and lay flat. Once 'trained', it will become more useable as you will not have to hold it down whilst trying to write in it.

Travel Checklist

Travel checklist inserts can be a simple list where you tick off items when you're packing for a trip. They're easy to create and develop, especially if you're a regular traveller. The time spent creating them can save you from forgetting vital items on a holiday or business trip.

Trifold

As the name implies, a 'tri-fold' was a wrap-around three-sided design of organiser. The two front 'sides' or covers overlapped each other and press studs held it in place.

The main advantage of this design was that it provided better protection to the outer edges of your pages.

The design was similar in size to a Duplex organiser, but where the second set of rings would be, instead this section could easily house two pen loops. To the right of this was an inside cover which, in the case of the Filofax Balmoral 10CLF J, held a jotter notepad. Overall, it was quite a large organiser fitted with 30mm rings.

The Filofax Balmoral 10 CLF J of this design dates to the late 1980's. However, we have seen similar design organisers made by Van der Spek as a custom order.

U

Undated Diary

Undated diary inserts allow you to note down information about appointments that will occur in the future beyond the date range of your current diary insert.

They can also be used to supplement your diary insert when you have a particularly busy week and you run out of space on your pages. You simply insert an undated page into your diary insert at the appropriate place.

Unlined Paper

Plain paper, sometimes coloured.

V

Van der Spek

A small family company based in the Netherlands that has been involved in making leather goods since 1926. The fourth generation of the family now heads the company. Petra and her family have expanded from just supplying local shops in the Netherlands to a worldwide online business since being 'discovered' by Janet Carr and Steve Morton in late 2013.

Van der Spek produces a full range of leather planner products, not only ring-bound organisers. They have a ready-to-ship range known as their 'Touch Me' range.

New products have been gradually added to the product line and sales have expanded beyond expectations.

They also provide custom-made leather planners and organisers which are hand made to order in their own workshop in the Netherlands from a vast range of different leathers in assorted colours.

It's fair to say that no two custom-made organisers are likely to be the same. They are very popular and produced to a very high standard. Complementing this, the family are able to provide an unrivalled level of customer service.

Website: https://www.vdsshop.com

Vintage Models

Older Filofax models didn't always have a model name as they do today. Instead, you will find a confusing set of letters and numbers to describe the design.

First digit(s) – The number of internal pockets
Next two Letters – Type of Leather:

- C – Canvas
- L – Leather cloth
- KL – Kid Leather
- CL – Calf Leather
- PL – Pigskin Leather
- HL – Hide Leather
- ML – Morocco Leather
- BCL – Box Calf Leather
- R – Rubberised
- RH – Reindeer Hide
- BL – Bridle Leather
- SH – Saddle Hide Leather
- CC – Crocodile Calf Leather
- V – Vinyl
- VR – Vinyl Rubber

Next position: F for fastener, J for Jotter, if present
Ring size in inches

An example: *Winchester 4CLF78* has four internal pockets, Calf Leather, Fastener and 7/8" rings (23mm)

Visual Reminders (stickers)

Stickers of graphical symbols or simple coloured dots can save space for writing, yet they can still serve as a visual reminder of appointments, days off, days when you must do a certain task each week. Some stickers can also be moved from one week to the next which helps keep your pages neat and tidy.

W

Washi Tape

A colourful paper self-adhesive tape. Washi paper originates from Japan, but it is now sold around the world.

The planner community adopted it in a large variety of designs to decorate diary inserts and other pages to show the creator's mood or the events of that week.

Westminster

The Filofax Westminster was an unusual double organiser and available as a Personal/Slimline or as an A5/Slimline pairing. It can be found in the 2000 Filofax catalogue.

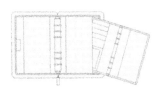 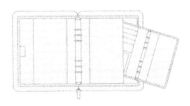

A similar arrangement can be created today with a Holborn A5 Zip and a Holborn Slimline.

William Hannah Ltd.

A small family company based in Leicestershire that produces A5 and A6 disc-bound notebook/planner covers in leather, as well as other leather items.

The packaging and overall finish of their products is exceptional and must be seen and experienced to fully appreciate their attention to detail that runs through the whole buying experience to when you receive and first open your purchase. There is a definite 'WOW' moment when you open the shipping package.

David Round has continued to work on developing the products with new models being offered from time to time. There are 'ready to ship' and bespoke models available in each model range.

William Hannah also offers a range of inserts for their notebooks for planning and general writing with your favourite fountain pens. The majority of their sales are through their website https://williamhannah.com. David also attends selected pen shows in UK.

World Information

Inserts are available that show information for other countries you might be visiting. Such information includes:

- Telephone number dialling codes
- Time zone maps
- City maps
- Telephone numbers for local enquiry offices for airlines, train services, car hire companies, etc.

X

Xafolif

Filofax spelt backwards!

Y

Year Planner

A diary insert that lets you see a full year on a single page. The boxes tend to be quite small, so colour coding of appointments and events is strongly recommended.

Yuppie

A fashionable young middle-class person with a well-paid job, in other words, a 'Young upwardly mobile professional' in the 1980s. The Filofax personal organiser was a perfect (and almost obligatory) accessory for this group.

Z

Z-Fold

A page that is folded twice to fit in to a regular size organiser.

Zen To Done by Leo Babauta (ZTD)

This book took the essentials of *Getting Things Done* by David Allen and simplified the productivity system in order to capture the essentials – focusing on carrying out tasks and reducing the stress of life with a set of simple habits.

Zipped Envelope

An insert to hold loose paperwork. It can be transparent plastic or made of strong paper and fits onto your organiser rings.

Zipped Organiser

Instead of a clasp and popper to keep the organiser fastened, a zipped organiser has a zip that closes it on three of the four sides. The advantage is that loose papers are less likely to fall out of the organiser. However, this is at the cost of the flexibility of opening the organiser quickly to jot something down so as to not forget it.

CHRONOLOGY OF FILOFAX

1796

John Letts founded his printing and book binding business in the Royal Exchange, London.

1812

The first Letts diary was launched. By the 1850s they were using the advertising slogan: 'Use your diary with the utmost familiarity and confidence. Conceal nothing from its pages nor suffer any other eye than your own to scan them.'

1910

Lefax company founded by J. C. Parker in Philadelphia.

1914-1918

British Army officer Colonel Disney working in the US came across a Lefax organiser and bought the idea over to UK with the aim of having it marketed there by a contact in London.

6 June 1921

The Norman & Hill company of printers and stationers was incorporated by the Rounce brothers in Appold Street in the City of London at the premises of W&T Rounce.

1921

Norman & Hill import personal filing systems from Lefax at the suggestion of Grace Scurr, the temporary secretary.

1925

The name Filofax was 'invented' by Grace Scurr.

1929

Norman & Hill offices at 40 Foster Lane, Cheapside, London EC2

1930

The Filofax trademark was registered.

1937

Norman & Hill offices at 16 Newgate Street, London EC1

30 December 1940

Norman & Hill offices, then in Aldersgate Street, were bombed.

1941

Norman & Hill moved to temporary offices in 47c Queens Road, Watford.

1941

Grace Scurr offered the position of manager of the company.

1955

Grace Scurr resigned as chairman of the company.

1955-1980

Joe Rider chairman of Norman & Hill

1976

David and Lesley Collischon started their own company 'Pocketfax' to sell the brand by mail.

1980

David and Lesley Collischon buy Norman & Hill and rename it Filofax

1980-1982

The Norman & Hill name was phased out to be replaced by Filofax with the now familiar logo *fILOFAX.*

10 December 1986

Norman & Hill officially became Filofax Ltd.

February 1988

Deskfax nine-ring launched, replacing the six-ring version.

1989

Four-ring Pocket organisers introduced.

1990

Company acquired by Transwood Earl.

October 1990

Robin Field appointed Chief Executive.

October 1992

Lefax bought by Filofax.

1992

A5 size launched. Products first appeared in the 1993 catalogue.

1993

Ilford workforce cut.

April 1994

Six-ring Pocket organisers introduced.

June 1995

Filofax Mini launched. Products first appeared in the late 1996 catalogue.

1997

Filofax moved their HQ to Burgess Hill, Sussex.

June 1998

David Collischon retired as executive chairman but stayed on as non-executive director. Robin Field replaced him.

October 1998

Day Runner acquired Filofax.

1998

Gordon Presly appointed Chief Executive.

2000

Filofax A4 size launched, effectively replacing the Deskfax size within a few years.

2001

M2 three-ring organisers launched.

July 2001

Filofax acquired by Letts, forming the Letts Filofax Group.

October 2005

Philofaxy blog created by 'Philofaxer'.

February 2006

Letts Filofax acquired by Phoenix Equity Partners.

2012

Filofax Compact size launched. Page size the same as Personal but generally 15mm ring size.

April 2013

Letts Filofax acquired by Chief Executive Gordon Presley and partner Harolde Savoy (HSGP investments). Letts Filofax now trading as Letts Filofax Blueline (LFB Group).

June 2014

Charles Letts died, aged 49. He had been the overseas sales manager for the Letts Filofax Group and was the last Letts in a long family history of the diary company dating back to 1796.

2015

Gordon Presly retired from Letts Filofax Blueline (LFB Group).

To be continued…

LIST OF MODELS AND YEARS

The following lists were supplied by Robert Mayr from Filowiki and were compiled from Filofax catalogues on Philofaxy and from other sources.

However, there may still be some models not included.

To the best of our knowledge, the years are accurate but we know that dates can vary by a year or two either way, depending on the model and the availability in different countries at the time.

Note: Some years will be covered on two pages.

Model	Year	Material
Billingham 4BLCF7/8	1978	Canvas and kid leather
Canvas 0C Personal	1980	Canvas
Duplex D2CLF Personal	1980	Calf leather
Gloucester 6CL Personal	1980	Montana calf leather
Leathercloth 0L Personal	1980	Faux leather
Marlborough 5CL Personal	1980	Calf leather
Slimline 3CL	1980	Leather
Winchester 5CLF Personal	1980	Leather
Slimline 3KL	1984	Kid leather
Slimline 3PL	1984	Pigskin leather
Winchester 4CLF Personal	1984	Leather
Winchester 4HLF Hide Leather Personal	1984	Hide leather
Ostrich (1st gen, 1980s) OLF Personal	1985	Genuine ostrich leather
Wellington 2RF7	1985	Rubberised outer cover
Winchester 4SLF Sharkskin	1985	Real Sharkskin leather
Balmoral 10CLF Karung	1986	Karung snake-leather
Balmoral 10CLF Personal	1986	Leather
Buckingham 2MLF Personal	1986	Moroccan leather
Buckingham 2PLF Personal	1986	Pigskin leather
Buckingham Personal	1986	Leather
Grosvenor 9KLF7/8	1986	Kid leather
Jazz Suite 2VF7/8	1986	Vinyl
Winchester 4PLF Pigskin	1986	No padding, stiffening material not identifiable
Winchester 4CCF King Crocodile Personal	1987	No padding, stiffening material not identifiable
Argyll 2CLF Personal	1988	Leather
Carmarthen 10BCLF7/8	1988	Box Calf Leather
Chicco OVF7/8	1988	Vinyl

Model	Year	Material
Durham 0CLF Personal	1988	Leather
Travelfax 14CLFZ Personal	1988	Calf leather
Zeppo OFF7/8	1988	Leather look
Buckingham 2BLF Personal	1989	Bridle leather
Statesman DX1CLF Deskfax	1989	Leather
Winchester 4CLF TS Tortoiseshell Personal	1989	Leather
Envoy DX0MLF Deskfax	1990	Moroccan leather
Envoy DX0VP/M Deskfax	1990	Vinyl
Iguana Pocket	1990	Leather with Iguana (lizard) print
Lincoln Personal	1990	Leather
Ostrich (2nd gen, 1990s) Personal	1990	Genuine ostrich leather
Ranger Personal	1990	Canvas
Sherwood Personal	1990	Scottish calf / alternative" (after 1993) leather"
Winchester 4CLF IG Iguana Personal	1990	No padding, stiffening material not identifiable
Cobra Personal	1991	Vinyl
College Personal	1991	Smooth suede-like vinyl
Devonshire Personal	1991	Deluxe smooth leather
Tejus Personal	1991	Leather with a lizard print
Berwick Personal	1992	Vinyl
Berwick Pocket	1992	Vinyl
Dundee Personal	1992	Stiffening material
Dundee Slimline	1992	Calf leather with crocodile print
Sherwood Pocket	1992	Deluxe smooth leather
Slimline	1992	Leather
Tejus Pocket	1992	Leather with a lizard print
Slimline Executive	1993	Leather
Windsor Personal	1993	Leather

1993-1996

Model	Year	Material
Windsor Pocket	1993	Leather
York Personal	1993	Natural vegetable tanned calf leather
Chester Personal tapestry	1994	Leather spine, leather trimmings, canvas-decoration like a tapestry, green suede-finish vinyl on the inside
Tejus Pocket Purse	1994	Leather with a lizard print
Windsor Lock Personal	1994	Grained leather interior leather combined with textile
Ascot A5	1996	Leather with crocodile print, leather on the inside
Ascot Personal	1996	Very high quality, no loss of material even after years of use
Ascot Pocket	1996	Very high quality, no loss of material even after years of use
Dorchester Personal	1996	Nubuck with brown leather spine
Keswick Personal	1996	Smooth stylish vinyl
Portland 5/4 Personal	1996	Leather
Portland Grand Personal	1996	Leather
Portland Personal	1996	Leather
Portland Pocket	1996	Leather
Richmond Personal	1996	Stiffening material
York A5	1996	Natural vegetable tanned calf leather
York Deskfax	1996	Natural vegetable tanned calf leather
York Pocket	1996	Natural vegetable tanned calf leather

Model	Year	Material
Connaught Personal	1998	Cardboard stiffening material identifiable
Piccadilly Personal	1998	Pebbled grained Italian leather cover with smooth leather interior
Richmond Deskfax	1998	Stiffening material
Richmond Slimline	1998	Grained leather
Savannah Personal	1998	Slight padding, cardboard stiffening material identifiable
Savannah Pocket	1998	Calf leather (ostrich print on the outside, smooth leather on the inside)
Brompton Personal	1999	Deluxe Leather
Brompton Pocket	1999	Deluxe Leather
Cavendish Compact	1999	Leather
Cavendish Mini	1999	Soft creamy leather
Cavendish Personal	1999	Leather
Cavendish Pocket	1999	Leather
Cosmic	1999	Faux leather
Grosvenor Mini	1999	Nappa leather
Grosvenor Pocket	1999	Nappa leather
Grosvenor Slimline	1999	Nappa leather
Hamilton A5	1999	Oiled leather
Hamilton Personal	1999	Oiled leather
Hamilton Personal ZIP	1999	Oiled leather
Hamilton Pocket	1999	Oiled leather
Henley Personal	1999	Foam padding, cardboard stiffening material identifiable
Henley Pocket	1999	Cow leather with faux basketweave finish
Kensington Deskfax	1999	Leather

1999-2001

Model	Year	Material
Kensington Mini	1999	Leather
Kensington Personal	1999	Leather
Kensington Pocket	1999	Leather
Kensington Slimline	1999	Leather
Kent A5	1999	Faux leather
Kent Deskfax	1999	Faux leather
Kent Personal	1999	faux leather
Kent Pocket	1999	Faux leather
Knightsbridge Personal	1999	Leather
Piccadilly Slimline	1999	Pebbled grained Italian leather cover with smooth leather interior
Sandhurst A5	1999	Padding not identifiable, stiffening material identifiable;
Sandhurst Mini	1999	Padding not identifiable, stiffening material identifiable;
Sandhurst Personal	1999	Padding not identifiable, stiffening material identifiable;
Sandhurst Pocket	1999	Padding not identifiable, stiffening material identifiable;
Sandhurst Slimline	1999	Calf leather, made in Italy
Westminster A5/Slimline	1999	Double organiser in leather
Westminster Personal/Slimline	1999	Double organiser in leather
Westminster Slimline	1999	Leather
Balmoral A5	2000	No padding, stiffening material identifiable
Balmoral Personal	2000	No padding, stiffening material identifiable
Alligator Personal	2001	Genuine alligator leather

2001-2003

Model	Year	Material
Balmoral M2	2001	Leather with a crocodile print
Balmoral Mini	2001	No padding, stiffening material not identifiable
Balmoral Pocket	2001	No padding, stiffening material identifiable
Bridle Personal	2001	Calf leather
Hamilton Pocket ZIP	2001	Oiled leather
Lizard Personal	2001	Genuine lizard leather
Ostrich (3rd gen, 2000s) Personal	2001	Genuine ostrich leather
Ostrich (3rd gen, 2000s) Pocket	2001	Genuine ostrich leather
Portobello Personal	2001	Soft leather on the outside and inside
Portobello Pocket	2001	Soft leather on the outside and inside
Ranger Personal	2001	Faux leather
Ranger Pocket	2001	Faux leather
Steel Personal	2001	Brushed metal effect synthetic
Belgravia A5	2002	Soft leather on the outside and inside
Belgravia Personal	2002	Soft leather on the outside and inside
Tecnic Personal	2002	Structured plastic
Finsbury (1st gen) Personal	2003	Outside: textured leather Inside: combination of exterior leather and matching lining
Finsbury Pocket	2003	Outside: textured leather Inside: combination of exterior leather and matching lining

2004-2005

Model	Year	Material
Belmont A5	2004	Italian calf leather
Belmont Personal	2004	Italian calf leather
Belmont Pocket	2004	Italian calf leather
Bloomsbury A5	2004	Soft leather on the outside and inside
Bloomsbury Pocket	2004	Soft leather on the outside and inside
Cross M2	2004	Leather
Denim Personal	2004	Textile
Denim Pocket	2004	Textile
Domino Personal	2004	Faux leather
Hampstead A5	2004	Oiled leather
Hampstead Personal	2004	Oiled leather
Metropol Mini	2004	Faux leather
Metropol Personal	2004	Faux leather
Metropol Personal ZIP	2004	Faux leather
Metropol Pocket	2004	Faux leather
Metropol Slimline	2004	Faux leather
Pimlico Personal	2004	Leather
Pimlico Pocket	2004	Leather
Topaz Mini	2004	Stiffening material not identifiable
Topaz Personal	2004	Stiffening material not identifiable
Topaz Pocket	2004	Leather with a very fine lizard print
Eton Personal	2005	Fine lambskin leather
Eton Pocket	2005	Fine lambskin leather
Eton Slimline	2005	Fine lambskin leather

2005-2006

Model	Year	Material
Finsbury (2nd gen) A5	2005	Outside: textured rambler print leather with hand finished colour Inside: combination of exterior leather and black lining
Finsbury (2nd gen) Mini	2005	Outside: textured rambler print leather with hand finished colour Inside: combination of exterior leather and black lining
Finsbury (2nd gen) Personal	2005	Outside: textured rambler print leather with hand finished colour Inside: combination of exterior leather and black lining
Finsbury (2nd gen) Personal ZIP	2005	Outside: textured rambler print leather with hand finished colour Inside: combination of exterior leather and black lining
Finsbury (2nd gen) Pocket	2005	Outside: textured rambler print leather with hand finished colour Inside: combination of exterior leather and black lining
Finsbury (2nd gen) Slimline	2005	Outside: textured rambler print leather with hand finished colour Inside: combination of exterior leather and black lining
Stratford Personal	2005	No padding, stiffening material not identifiable
Waverley Personal	2005	Fine lambskin leather
Chino Personal	2006	Soft-brushed textile
Classic A5	2006	Padding, stiffening material very identifiable

2006-2008

Model	Year	Material
Classic Compact	2006	Padding, stiffening material very identifiable
Classic Mini	2006	Padding, stiffening material very identifiable
Classic Personal	2006	Padding, stiffening material very identifiable
Classic Pocket	2006	Padding, stiffening material very identifiable
Eden Personal	2006	Textile
Eton 85th Anniversary Personal	2006	Fine lambskin leather, '85' print on the front
Amazona A5	2008	Leather with crocodile print
Finchley A5	2006	Padding, stiffening material identifiable
Finchley Mini	2006	Padding, stiffening material identifiable
Finchley Personal	2006	Padding, stiffening material identifiable
Finchley Pocket	2006	Padding, stiffening material identifiable
Kendal A5	2006	Oiled leather
Kendal Mini	2006	Oiled leather
Kendal Personal	2006	Oiled leather
Kendal Pocket	2006	Oiled leather
Kendal Slimline	2006	Oiled leather
Piazza Mini	2006	Deluxe smooth leather
Rio Personal	2006	Italian textile on the inside
Amazona Mini	2008	Leather with crocodile print
Amazona Personal	2008	Leather with crocodile print
Amazona Pocket	2008	Leather with crocodile print
Baroque Mini	2008	Smooth leather on the outside, 'baroque'-style print on the inside;

Model	Year	Material
Baroque Personal	2008	Smooth leather on the outside, 'baroque'-style print on the inside;
Baroque Pocket	2008	Smooth leather on the outside, 'baroque'-style print on the inside;
Botanic Personal	2008	Canvas-decoration (textile)
Botanic Pocket	2008	Canvas-decoration (textile)
Breast Cancer Campaign Personal	2008	Faux leather
Cuban A5	2008	Italian leather
Cuban A5 ZIP	2008	Italian leather
Cuban Personal	2008	Italian leather
Cuban Personal ZIP	2008	Italian leather
Cuban Pocket	2008	Italian leather
Cuban Slimline	2008	Italian leather
Deco Personal	2008	Leather with crocodile print, suede leather on the inside
Deco Pocket	2008	Leather with crocodile print, suede leather on the inside
Graphic Personal	2008	Plastic
Graphic Personal ZIP	2008	Plastic
Guildford A5	2008	Soft leather
Guildford Mini	2008	Soft leather
Guildford Mini Extra Slim	2008	No padding, stiffening material not identifiable
Guildford Personal	2008	Soft leather
Guildford Personal ZIP	2008	Soft leather
Guildford Pocket	2008	Soft leather
Guildford Slimline	2008	No padding, stiffening material not identifiable
Ikon A5	2008	Bonded leather

Model	Year	Material
Panama Personal	2008	Leather on the outside with beige-coloured leather on the inside
Panama Pocket	2008	Leather on the outside with beige-coloured leather on the inside
Siena A5	2008	Leather
Siena Personal	2008	Leather
Urban Personal	2008	Faux leather
Urban Pocket	2008	Faux leather
Adelphi A5	2009	Deluxe leather with print
Adelphi Personal	2009	Deluxe leather with print
Adelphi Pocket	2009	Deluxe leather with print
Butterfly Personal	2009	Leather
Butterfly Pocket	2009	Leather
Fresco Personal	2009	Textile
Fresco Pocket	2009	Textile
Indie Personal	2009	Textile
Hearts Personal	2010	Cardboard stiffening material identifiable
Amazona Slimline	2011	Leather with crocodile print
Apex A5	2011	Structured plastic
Apex Pocket	2011	Structured plastic
Aston Personal	2011	Soft small grained leather
Aston Pocket	2011	Soft small grained leather
Chameleon A5	2011	Leather with lizard print
Chameleon Compact	2011	Leather with lizard print
Chameleon Mini	2011	Leather with lizard print
Chameleon Personal	2011	Leather with lizard print
Chameleon Pocket	2011	Leather with lizard print
Deco Slimline	2011	Leather with crocodile print, suede leather on the inside

2011-2011

Model	Year	Material
Holborn A5	2011	Soft buffalo-leather with unobtrusive grain Interior leather combined with textile
Holborn Compact	2011	Soft buffalo-leather with unobtrusive grain Interior leather combined with textile
Holborn Personal	2011	Soft buffalo-leather with unobtrusive grain Interior leather combined with textile
Holborn Personal ZIP	2011	Soft buffalo-leather with unobtrusive grain Interior leather combined with textile
Holborn Pocket	2011	Soft buffalo-leather with unobtrusive grain Interior leather combined with textile
Holborn Slimline	2011	Soft buffalo-leather with unobtrusive grain Interior leather combined with textile
Luxe A5	2011	Leather
Luxe Compact	2011	Leather
Malden Personal	2011	Leather, no padding, stiffening material not identifiable
Malden Pocket	2011	Leather, no padding, stiffening material not identifiable
Osterley A5	2011	Leather with sleek crocodile print and sleek leather
Osterley Compact	2011	Leather with sleek crocodile print and sleek leather

2011-2012

Model	Year	Material
Osterley Personal	2011	Leather with sleek crocodile print and sleek leather
Scanda Personal	2011	Used-look leather with contrast stitching
Sketch Personal	2011	Padding, stiffening material identifiable
Sketch Personal ZIP	2011	Plastic
Songbird Personal	2011	Textile
Aston A5	2012	Soft small grained leather
Domino Mix Personal	2012	Faux leather
Domino Mix Pocket	2012	Faux leather
Domino Snake A5	2012	Faux leather
Domino Snake Personal	2012	Faux leather
Fusion A5	2012	Polyester microfibre textile, black full grain leather;
Fusion Personal	2012	Polyester microfibre textile, black full grain leather;
Jack Vintage Personal	2012	Faux leather
London 2012 Line Burst Personal	2012	Faux leather
London 2012 Line Burst Pocket	2012	Faux leather
London 2012 Sporting Icons Personal	2012	Plastic
Malden A5	2012	Leather, no padding, stiffening material not identifiable
Malden Mini	2012	Leather, no padding, stiffening material not identifiable
Pennybridge A5 ZIP	2012	Faux leather; textured;

2012-2016

Model	Year	Material
Pennybridge Compact ZIP	2012	Faux leather: black and red have been available as smooth and textured, other colours are textured
Pennybridge Pocket ZIP	2012	Faux leather; black and red have been available as smooth and textured, other colours are textured;
Swift Personal	2012	Textile outside, green textile/plastic inside
Back to School Compact	2013	Faux leather
Boston Compact	2013	Full-grain nappa leather
Calipso A5	2013	Leather, interior textile-leather-mix
Calipso Compact	2013	Leather, interior textile-leather-mix
Malden Compact ZIP	2013	Leather, no padding, stiffening material not identifiable
Malden Pocket Zip	2013	Leather, no padding, stiffening material not identifiable
Original A5	2013	Leather
Original Personal	2013	Leather
Saffiano Personal	2013	Faux leather with cross-grain
Temperley Ikat Compact	2013	Printed canvas
Temperley Violet Compact	2013	Italian calf leather with crocodile print
The Journey Travel Companion	2013	Leather
The Purse Compact Zip	2013	Leather
Cover Story Flamingo Personal	2014	Textile outside, green textile/plastic inside
Domino Patent Personal	2016	Faux leather

2016-2019

Model	Year	Material
Lockwood A5 ZIP	2016	Deluxe full grain leather
Lockwood Personal ZIP	2016	Deluxe full grain leather
Heritage Compact A5	2016	Premium Leather
Heritage Personal	2016	Premium Leather
Heritage Compact Personal	2016	Premium Leather
Heritage Slimline	2016	Premium Leather
Classic Croc A5	2016	Italian Calf Leather
Classic Croc Personal	2016	Italian Calf Leather
Classic Croc Pocket	2016	Italian Calf Leather
Classic Stitch Soft A5	2016	Soft full grain leather
Classic Stitch Soft Personal	2016	Soft full grain leather
Classic Stitch Soft Pocket	2016	Soft full grain leather
Lockwood A5	2017	Deluxe full grain leather
Lockwood Personal	2017	Deluxe full grain leather
Lockwood Personal Slim	2017	Deluxe full grain leather
Lockwood Pocket	2017	Deluxe full grain leather
Chester Compact A5	2019	Luxury Italian leather
Chester Personal Slim	2019	Luxury Italian leather
Chester Personal	2019	Luxury Italian leather

WOULD YOU LEAVE A REVIEW?

I hope you enjoyed this *fILE OF fACTS.*
If you did, I'd really appreciate it if you would write a few words
of review on the site where you purchased this book.

Reviews help books to feature more prominently on retailer sites
and invite more readers to find out about the world of organisers.

Thank you so much!

ACKNOWLEDGEMENTS

Petra Van der Spek of Van der Spek Leather Goods for her encouragement and permission to use a Van der Spek organiser as the cover image.

Robert Mayr for his FiloWiki site and for supplying the Filofax model list in this book.

Max Greengrass for his assistance in investigating some of the historical facts about Filofax.

Nan Barber for her courage in offering me a chance to join her on Philofaxy in 2009.

David Round of William Hannah Ltd for encouraging me to finish writing this book.

Cathy Helms of Avalon Graphics for her patience and professionalism for designing the cover and fending off my wackier ideas.

Janet Carr for her stalwart beta-reading

Alison Morton, experienced author-publisher (and my wife!) who knocked my text into order and published it under her imprint, Pulcheria Press.

CPSIA information can be obtained
at www.ICGtesting.com
Printed in the USA
LVHW012305161221
706400LV00015B/418